Fairy Cooking

Rebecca Gilpin and Catherine Atkinson

Designed by Nicola Butler
Illustrated by Molly Sage
Photographs by Howard Allman

Americanization: Carrie Seay
American expert: Barbara Tricinella

Contents

Spangly heart cookies

To make about 25 cookies, you will need:

2 tablespoons granulated sugar
red food coloring
6 tablespoons (3 oz.) butter, softened
3 tablespoons light brown sugar
3 tablespoons maple syrup
1 medium egg
1½ cups all-purpose flour
a medium and a small heart-shaped cutter
two greased cookie sheets

Preheat your oven to 350°F.

✿ The cookies need to be stored in an airtight container and eaten within a week.

Add one spoonful of maple syrup at a time.

1. Put the granulated sugar in a bowl, add two drops of coloring and stir the sugar until it is pink. Then, spread it out on a plate to dry.

2. Put the butter and brown sugar into a large bowl. Stir them hard until they are creamy, then stir in the maple syrup.

3. Carefully break the egg into a small bowl, then pour it slowly onto a saucer. Then, put a cup over the yolk.

Keep the egg white.

4. Hold the cup over the yolk and carefully tip the saucer over the small bowl so that the egg white dribbles into it.

5. Add the yolk to the large bowl and mix it in. Add the flour and stir it in well, then squeeze the mixture to make a dough.

6. Wrap the dough in plastic food wrap and put it in the refrigerator to chill for half an hour. While it is in there, turn on your oven.

7. Sprinkle a clean work surface with flour. Then, use a rolling pin to roll out the dough until it is about ¼ inch thick.

8. Use the medium cutter to cut out heart shapes. Then, lift the hearts onto the cookie sheets with a spatula.

9. Cut holes in the hearts with the small cutter. Then, make the scraps into a ball, roll them out and cut out more hearts.

Wear oven mitts.

10. Using a fork, stir the egg white quickly for a few seconds. Brush some onto each cookie, then sprinkle them with pink sugar.

11. Bake the cookies for 10-12 minutes, until they start to turn golden brown. Then, carefully lift them out of the oven.

12. Leave the cookies on the cookie sheets for a few minutes. Then, lift them onto a wire rack and leave them to cool.

Pretty fairy fudge

To make about 70 fudge shapes, you will need:

1lb. box powdered sugar
about 16 (4 oz.) pink jumbo marshmallows
2 tablespoons milk
½ cup (1 stick) unsalted butter
½ teaspoon of vanilla
red food coloring
small cutters
small candies, for decorating

✿ The fudge needs to be stored in an airtight container in the refrigerator and eaten within a week.

1. Sift the powdered sugar through a sifter into a large bowl. Make a small hollow in the middle of the sugar with a spoon.

2. Using clean scissors, cut the marshmallows in half and put them in a small pan. Add the milk, butter and vanilla.

3. Gently heat the pan. Stir the mixture every now and then with a wooden spoon until everything has just melted.

4. Pour the mixture into the hollow in the sugar. Mix everything together until it is smooth, then mix in a drop of coloring.

5. Leave the mixture to cool for 10 minutes, then make it into a flattened round shape. Then, wrap it in plastic food wrap.

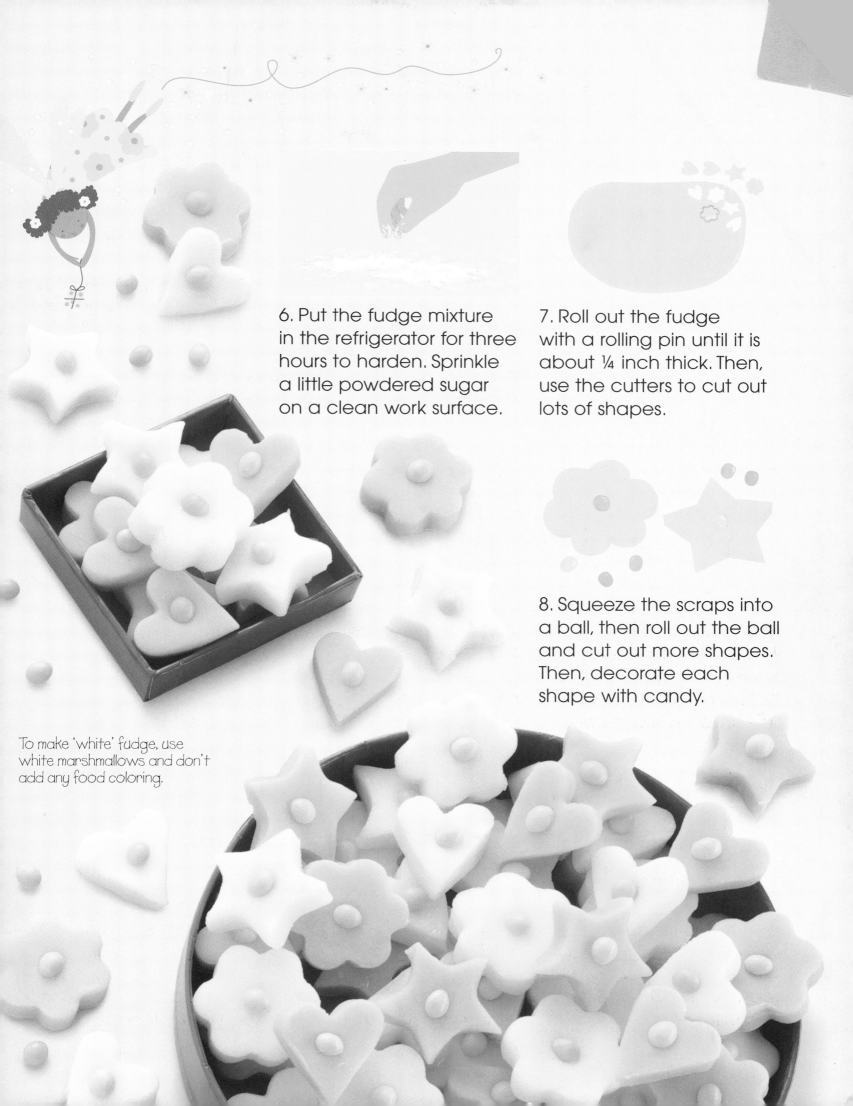

6. Put the fudge mixture in the refrigerator for three hours to harden. Sprinkle a little powdered sugar on a clean work surface.

7. Roll out the fudge with a rolling pin until it is about ¼ inch thick. Then, use the cutters to cut out lots of shapes.

8. Squeeze the scraps into a ball, then roll out the ball and cut out more shapes. Then, decorate each shape with candy.

To make 'white' fudge, use white marshmallows and don't add any food coloring.

Fairy muffins

To make 10 muffins, you will need:

2½ cups all-purpose flour
2 teaspoons baking powder
¾ cup granulated sugar
1 lemon
4 tablespoons butter
1 cup milk
1 medium egg
½ cup (4 oz.) seedless raspberry preserves
a 12-hole muffin tray
small candies and sugar strands, for decorating

For the icing:
1½ cups powdered sugar
2 tablespoons lemon juice squeezed from
   the lemon from the main mixture

Preheat your oven to 400°F.

❁ The muffins need to be stored in an airtight container and should be eaten on the day you make them.

Use a pastry brush.

If you are having a birthday party, you could decorate some of the muffins with little candles.

1. Brush some oil in ten of the muffin holes. Then, cut a small circle of baking parchment to put in the bottom of each hole.

2. Sift the flour and baking powder into a large bowl. Add the granulated sugar, then mix everything with a metal spoon.

Use a lemon squeezer.

3. Grate the rind from the lemon using the medium holes on a grater. Then, cut the lemon in half and squeeze the juice from it.

4. Put two tablespoons of juice on one side, for the icing. Then, cut the butter into pieces and put it in a pan with the lemon rind.

5. Add four tablespoons of milk and heat the pan until the butter melts. Then, take it off the heat and add the rest of the milk.

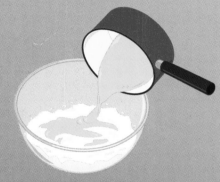

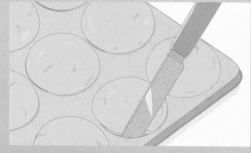

6. Break the egg into a cup and mix it well with a fork, then stir it into the butter mixture. Then, add the mixture to the bowl.

7. Stir everything together with a fork. Then, nearly fill each muffin hole with the mixture and bake the muffins for 15 minutes.

8. Leave the muffins in the tray for three minutes, then loosen them with a blunt knife. Then, put them on a wire rack to cool.

Use a sharp knife.

9. Turn each muffin on its side and cut it in half. Then, spread preserves on the bottom half and lay the top half on top.

10. Sift the powdered sugar into a bowl and mix in the lemon juice. Spoon icing onto the muffins. Press on some candies.

Swirly pink cookies

To make about 40 cookies, you will need:

$^2/_3$ cup powdered sugar
10 tablespoons butter, softened
1 lemon
1¾ cup all-purpose flour
2 tablespoons milk
red food coloring
two greased cookie sheets

Preheat your oven to 350°F.

✿ The cookies need to be stored in an airtight container and eaten within a week.

1. Using a sifter, sift the powdered sugar into a large bowl. Add the butter and mix it in until the mixture is creamy.

2. Grate the rind from a lemon using the fine holes on a grater. Then, add the rind to the creamy mixture and stir it in.

3. Put half of the mixture in another bowl. Sift half of the flour into each bowl, then add a tablespoon of milk to each one.

4. Add one to two drops of coloring to one of the bowls. Then, squeeze each mixture to make two balls of dough.

5. Flatten the balls of dough a little and wrap them in plastic food wrap. Put them in the refrigerator for 30 minutes to chill.

6. Sprinkle flour on a clean work surface, then roll out the plain dough until it is about 6 x 10 and ¼ inch thick.

7. Roll out the pink dough until it is about the same size as the plain dough. Then, brush the plain dough with a little water.

8. Carefully lift the pink dough and lay it on the plain dough. Then, use a sharp knife to make the edges straight.

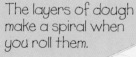

The layers of dough make a spiral when you roll them.

Use a spatula.

9. Roll up the dough from one of the long sides. Wrap it in plastic food wrap and chill it in the refrigerator for 30 minutes.

10. Turn on your oven. Then, cut the rolled-up dough into ¼ inch slices and put the slices on the cookie sheets.

11. Bake the cookies for 12-15 minutes. Leave them on the cookie sheets for two minutes, then lift them onto a wire rack to cool.

Mini fairy pastries

To make 24 pastries, you will need:

13-15 oz. package of ready-rolled puff pastry
1 medium red onion
1 tablespoon of olive oil
a pinch of salt and of ground black pepper
½ teaspoon of Italian seasonings
1 cup (5 oz.) grated mozzarella cheese
12 small cherry tomatoes, washed
1 tablespoon of milk
2 cookie sheets

Preheat your oven to 425°F.

✿ Leave the pastries to cool for five minutes, before you eat them.

1. Take the pastry out of the refrigerator and leave it out for 15-20 minutes. Then, carefully cut the ends off the onion.

2. Peel the onion and cut it in half. Then, cut each half into two pieces. Very carefully cut each piece into thin slices.

3. Gently heat the olive oil in a frying pan. Then, add the onion and stir it every now and then for about five minutes.

4. Remove the pan from the heat and stir in the salt, pepper and seasonings. Then, unroll the pastry and cut it into 24 squares.

5. Put the squares on the cookie sheets, leaving spaces between them. Prick the middle of each square twice with a fork.

6. On a chopping board, carefully cut the cherry tomatoes in half with a sharp knife. Put the cheese on the board too.

7. Pour the milk into a mug. Then, brush milk around the edge of each square, making a border about ½ inch wide.

8. Spoon some of the onion and herb mixture onto each square, making sure you don't cover the milk border.

Use a spatula to remove them.

9. Put half a tomato on the top of each square, then sprinkle grated mozzarella on the top of each one.

10. Cook the pastries for 12-15 minutes. When the edges have risen and turned brown, the pastries are cooked.

Pretty fairy star cookies

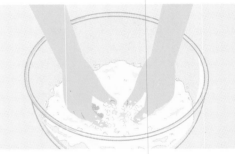

To make about 25 cookies, you will need:

2 cups all-purpose flour
2 teaspoons ground ginger
2 teaspoons baking soda
½ cup butter
¾ cup granulated sugar
¾ cup brown sugar

1 medium egg
4 tablespoons maple syrup
writing icing
small candy, for decorating
a large star-shaped cookie cutter
2 greased cookie sheets

Preheat your oven to 375°F.

❋ The cookies need to be stored in a single layer in an airtight container and eaten within five days.

1. Sift the flour into a large bowl. Then, sift the ground ginger and baking soda into the bowl too.

2. Cut the butter into chunks with a blunt knife. Then, add it to the bowl and stir it in so that it is coated with the flour.

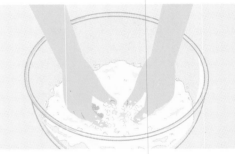

3. Rub the butter into the flour with your fingers until the mixture is like fine breadcrumbs. Then, stir in the sugar and brown sugar.

4. Break the egg into a small bowl, then add the syrup. Beat them together well with a fork, then stir the mixture into the flour.

5. Mix everything together until you make a dough. Then, sprinkle a clean work surface with flour and put the dough onto it.

6. Using your hands, push the dough away from you and fold it over. Do this again and again until the dough is smooth.

7. Sprinkle more flour onto the work surface, then roll out the dough until it is ¼ inch thick. Use the cutter to cut out stars.

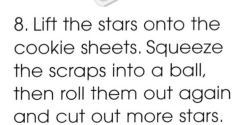

8. Lift the stars onto the cookie sheets. Squeeze the scraps into a ball, then roll them out again and cut out more stars.

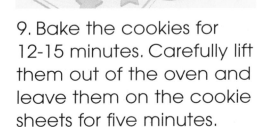

The cookies will be golden.

9. Bake the cookies for 12-15 minutes. Carefully lift them out of the oven and leave them on the cookie sheets for five minutes.

Stick on single candies with a dot of icing.

10. Put the cookies onto a wire rack to cool. When they are cold, decorate them with writing icing and press on small candies.

Flowery cut-out cookies

To make about 10 cookies, you will need:

½ cup (1 stick) butter, softened
¼ cup granulated sugar
a small orange
1 medium egg
2 tablespoons finely-ground almonds*
1¾ cups all-purpose flour

1 tablespoon of cornmeal
8 tablespoons raspberry preserves
a 2 inch round cookie cutter
a small flower cookie cutter
2 greased cookie sheets

Preheat your oven to 350°F.

❀ The cookies need to be eaten on the day you make them.

* Don't give these cookies to anyone who is allergic to nuts.

1. Put the butter and sugar into a large bowl. Mix them together with a wooden spoon until the mixture looks creamy.

2. Grate the rind from the orange using the medium holes on a grater. Then, add the rind to the bowl and stir it in.

3. Break the egg into a cup and mix it with a fork. Then, add a little of the egg to the creamy mixture and mix it in well.

4. Add some more egg to the bowl and mix it in. Continue until you have added all the egg, then add the ground almonds.

5. Put the flour and cornmeal into the bowl. Then, mix everything with your hands until you have made a dough.

6. Wrap the dough in plastic food wrap and put it in a refrigerator to chill for 30 minutes. While it is in there, turn on your oven.

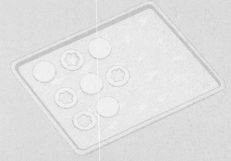

7. Sprinkle some flour onto a clean work surface. Then, use a rolling pin to roll out the dough until it is about 1/8 inch thick.

8. Using the round cutter, cut out lots of circles. Then, use the flower cutter to cut holes in the middle of half of the circles.

9. Squeeze the scraps into a ball. Then, roll out the ball and cut out more circles. Put all the circles on the cookie sheets.

The cookies turn golden brown.

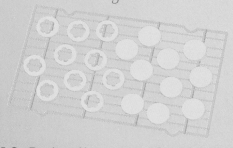

10. Bake the cookies for 15 minutes. Leave them on the cookie sheets for two minutes, then move them onto a wire rack to cool.

11. Spread preserves on the whole cookies, as far as the edge. Then, place a flower cookie on each one and press it down gently.

Tiny fairy cakes

To make about 20-24 fairy cakes, you will need:

1 medium egg
7 tablespoons self-rising flour
3 tablespoons butter, softened
3 tablespoons and 1 teaspoon
  granulated sugar
small paper candy cups
a cookie sheet

Preheat your oven to 350°F.

❀ The cakes need to be stored in
   an airtight container and eaten
   within four days.

For the icing:
½ cup powdered sugar
about 1 tablespoon of warm water
red food coloring
small candies and sugar sprinkles,
  for decorating

Use a wooden spoon.

1. Break the egg into a mug. Then, sift the flour into a large bowl and add the egg, butter and sugar.

2. Stir everything together well, until the mixture is smooth and creamy. Then, put 24 paper cups on the cookie sheet.

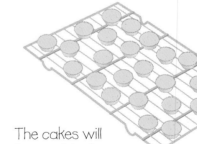

The cakes will turn golden brown.

3. Using a teaspoon, spoon the cake mixture into the paper cups until each case is just under half full.

4. Bake the cakes for about 10 minutes, then carefully take them out of the oven. Lift them onto a wire rack to cool.

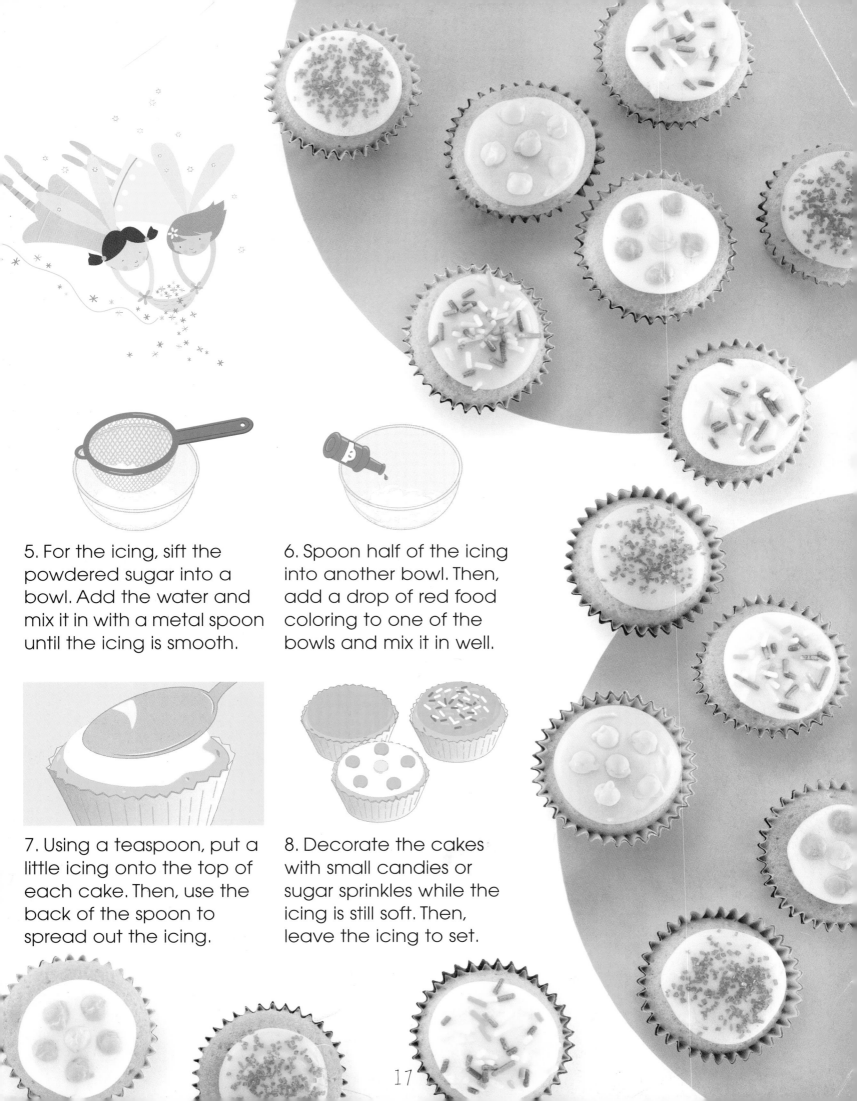

5. For the icing, sift the powdered sugar into a bowl. Add the water and mix it in with a metal spoon until the icing is smooth.

6. Spoon half of the icing into another bowl. Then, add a drop of red food coloring to one of the bowls and mix it in well.

7. Using a teaspoon, put a little icing onto the top of each cake. Then, use the back of the spoon to spread out the icing.

8. Decorate the cakes with small candies or sugar sprinkles while the icing is still soft. Then, leave the icing to set.

Iced raspberry mousse

To make 4 mousses, you will need:

a small box (6 oz. tub) raspberries
4 tablespoons powdered sugar, sifted
4 tablespoons vanilla yogurt
½ cup whipping cream
4-5 meringues*
fresh raspberries and small mint leaves,
  to decorate
four ½ cup ramekin dishes

❁ The mousses need to be stored in a freezer and eaten as soon as you have decorated them.

1. Put the raspberries in a bowl and mash them with a fork until they are squashed. Then, add the powdered sugar.

2. Stir the raspberries and powdered sugar to mix them. Then, add the yogurt and stir it in until everything is mixed well.

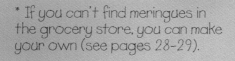

* If you can't find meringues in the grocery store, you can make your own (see pages 28-29).

18

Use a whisk or an egg beater.

3. Pour the cream into a bowl. Then, whisk the cream until it is thick and there are points when you lift the whisk or egg beater.

4. Add the yogurt mixture to the cream. Then, gently turn the mixture over and over with a spoon, to mix everything together.

5. Continue until the whole mixture is pink. Then, break the meringues into small pieces. Add them to the mixture and stir them in.

6. Spoon the mixture into the dishes. Then, put the dishes into a freezer for two hours, or until the mousses have frozen solid.

7. Take the frozen mousses out of the freezer. Then, decorate each mousse with a raspberry and two mint leaves.

Cut-out sandwiches

To make 3 sandwiches, you will need:

6 slices of bread
butter, softened
thin slices of ham
a cucumber
strawberry, raspberry or apricot preserves
a large round cookie cutter and a small cookie cutter

❀ Eat the sandwiches as soon as you've made them, or wrap them in plastic food wrap and store them in the refrigerator for up to six hours.

Ham sandwich

1. Lay a slice of bread on a chopping board. Place the round cutter on it and press hard. Then, remove the cut-out circle.

2. Cut another circle from a second slice of bread. Then, use the small cutter to cut a shape in one of the circles.

3. Lay the round cutter on top of a slice of ham. Then, very carefully cut around the cutter with a sharp knife.

4. Spread butter on one side of each bread circle. Then, lay the ham on the whole circle and lay the circle with the hole on top.

If you're having a party, make lots of sandwiches in different shapes and with different fillings.

Cucumber sandwich

1. Cut two bread circles and cut a hole in one of them. Then, slice the cucumber until you have lots of thin slices.

2. Spread butter on the bread circles and lay slices of cucumber on the whole one. Then, lay the circle with the hole on top.

Preserves

Cut two bread circles and cut a hole in one of them. Spread butter and preserves on the whole one, then press the circles together.

Chocolate cobweb cookies

To make about 18 cookies, you will need:

1⅓ cups all-purpose flour
3 tablespoons cocoa powder
½ cup (1 stick) butter, refrigerated
½ cup granulated sugar
2 tablespoons milk
white writing icing
a 2½ inch round cookie cutter
2 cookie sheets sprayed with non-stick cooking spray
   or lined with baking parchment
a toothpick

Preheat your oven to 350°F.

❀ The cookies need to be stored in a single layer in an airtight container and eaten within five days.

1. Put the flour and cocoa into a large bowl. Cut the butter into chunks and add it to the bowl, then rub it in with your fingers.

2. When the mixture looks like fine breadcrumbs, stir in the sugar. Then, sprinkle the milk over the mixture and stir it with a fork.

3. Stir the mixture until everything starts to stick together. Then, squeeze it with your hands to make a ball of dough.

Make a squashed circle.

4. Wrap the dough in plastic food wrap. Put it in a refrigerator for 20 minutes. While it is in there, turn on your oven.

The flour keeps the dough from sticking.

5. Sprinkle a clean work surface and a rolling pin with some flour. Then, roll out the dough until it is about ¼ inch thick.

6. Use the cutter to cut out lots of circles and carefully lift them onto the cookie sheets. Then, make the scraps into a ball.

Wear oven mitts.

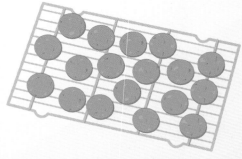

7. Roll out the ball and cut out more circles. Bake the cookies for about 12-15 minutes, then carefully lift them out of the oven.

8. Leave the cookies on the cookie sheets for about five minutes. Then, lift them onto a wire rack and leave them to cool.

9. Draw a spiral of white writing icing on each cookie, starting in the middle and working out toward the edge.

10. Using a toothpick, drag the icing from the middle to make a web. Ice the other cookies then leave the icing to set.

Butterfly cupcakes

To make 8 cupcakes, you will need:

1 medium egg
7 tablespoons self-rising flour
¼ teaspoon of baking powder
¼ cup granulated sugar
¼ cup butter, softened
paper baking cups
a muffin tray with shallow pans

Preheat your oven to 375°F.

❀ The cupcakes need to be eaten on the day you make them.

For the butter icing:
4 tablespoons butter, softened
a few drops vanilla
¾ cup and 2 tablespoons
    powdered sugar, sifted
about 4 teaspoons seedless
    raspberry preserves
extra powdered sugar, for dusting

1. Break the egg into a mug. Then, sift the flour and baking powder into a large bowl. Add the sugar, egg and butter.

2. Stir all the ingredients together with a wooden spoon. Continue until you have made a smooth creamy mixture.

3. Put eight baking cups into the pans in the muffin tray. Then, use a teaspoon to half fill each cup with the mixture.

Wear oven mitts.

4. Bake the cupcakes for 15-18 minutes. Then, carefully lift them out of the oven and put them on a wire rack to cool.

Use a wooden spoon.

5. To make the icing, put the butter into a bowl and add the vanilla. Stir them together until the mixture is really creamy.

6. Add some of the powdered sugar to the butter and stir it in. Repeat this until you have mixed in all the powdered sugar.

Leave an edge around the circle.

7. Using a sharp knife, carefully cut a circle from the top of each cupcake. Then, cut each circle in half, across the middle.

8. Spread some of the icing on top of each cupcake. Then, spoon half a teaspoon of preserves in a line across the icing.

9. Gently push two of the half slices into the icing, so that they look like wings. Then, sift a little powdered sugar over the top.

Little cheese scones

To make about 16 scones, you will need:

1/3 cup Cheddar cheese
1 2/3 cups self-rising flour
1/2 level teaspoon of baking powder
a pinch of salt
2 tablespoons butter
1/2 cup milk
milk, for glazing
1 1/2 inch round and heart-shaped cutters
a greased cookie sheet

Preheat your oven to 425°F.

✿ Eat the scones warm or store them in an airtight container
and eat them within three days.

Eat the scones
as they are or cut
them in half and spread
them with a little butter.

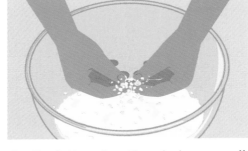

1. Grate the cheese using the medium holes on a grater. Then, sift the flour, baking powder and salt into a large bowl.

2. Cut the butter into small pieces and add them to the bowl. Then, rub them in until the mixture looks like fine breadcrumbs.

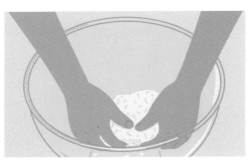

3. Mix in the grated cheese with your hands and pour in the milk. Then, use a blunt knife to mix everything together well.

4. Gently press the mixture together with your hands to make a soft dough. Then, sprinkle flour onto a clean work surface.

5. Using a rolling pin, roll out the dough until it is about ½ inch thick. Then, use the cutters to cut out circles and hearts.

6. Squeeze the leftover scraps of dough into a ball and roll them out again. Cut out more circles and hearts.

7. Put the shapes on the cookie sheet, leaving spaces between them. Then, brush the tops of them with a little milk.

Some of these scones had a little flour or grated cheese sprinkled onto them, before they were baked.

8. Bake the scones for seven to eight minutes, until they rise and turn golden. Then, lift them onto a wire rack to cool.

Mini meringues

To make about 15 white and 15 pink mini meringues, you will need:

2 large eggs, at room temperature
½ cup ultra-fine granulated sugar
red food coloring
½ cup heavy cream
2 cookie sheets sprayed with non-stick cooking spray
    or lined with baking parchment

Preheat your oven to 225°F.

❁ The meringues need to be stored in an airtight container and eaten within a week. Once you have filled them, eat them on the same day.

You could use a yolk to make confetti cookies (see pages 30–31).

1. Carefully break one egg on the edge of a small bowl, then pour it slowly onto a saucer. Put a cup over the yolk.

2. Hold the cup over the yolk and carefully tip the saucer over the bowl so that the egg white dribbles into it.

3. Repeat these steps with the other egg, so that the two egg whites are in the bowl. You don't need the yolks in this recipe.

4. Whisk the egg whites with a whisk or egg beater until they are really thick. They should form stiff points when you lift the whisk up.

5. Add a heaped teaspoon of sugar to the egg whites and whisk it in well. Repeat this until you have added all the sugar.

6. Scoop up a teaspoon of the meringue mixture. Then, use another teaspoon to push it off onto the cookie sheet.

7. Make 15 meringues, leaving gaps between them. Then, add two drops of food coloring to the rest of the mixture.

Use a metal spoon.

8. Gently mix in the food coloring by turning the mixture over slowly. Then, when the mixture is pink, make 15 more meringues.

9. Put the meringues in the oven and bake them for 30-40 minutes. Then, turn off the oven, leaving the meringues inside.

Wear oven mitts.

10. After 15 minutes, carefully lift the cookie sheets out of the oven. Leave the meringues on the trays to cool.

11. Pour the cream into a small bowl, then strongly whisk it with a whisk. Carry on until the cream is quite thick.

12. Using a blunt knife, spread some cream on the flat side of a meringue. Then, press another meringue on the top.

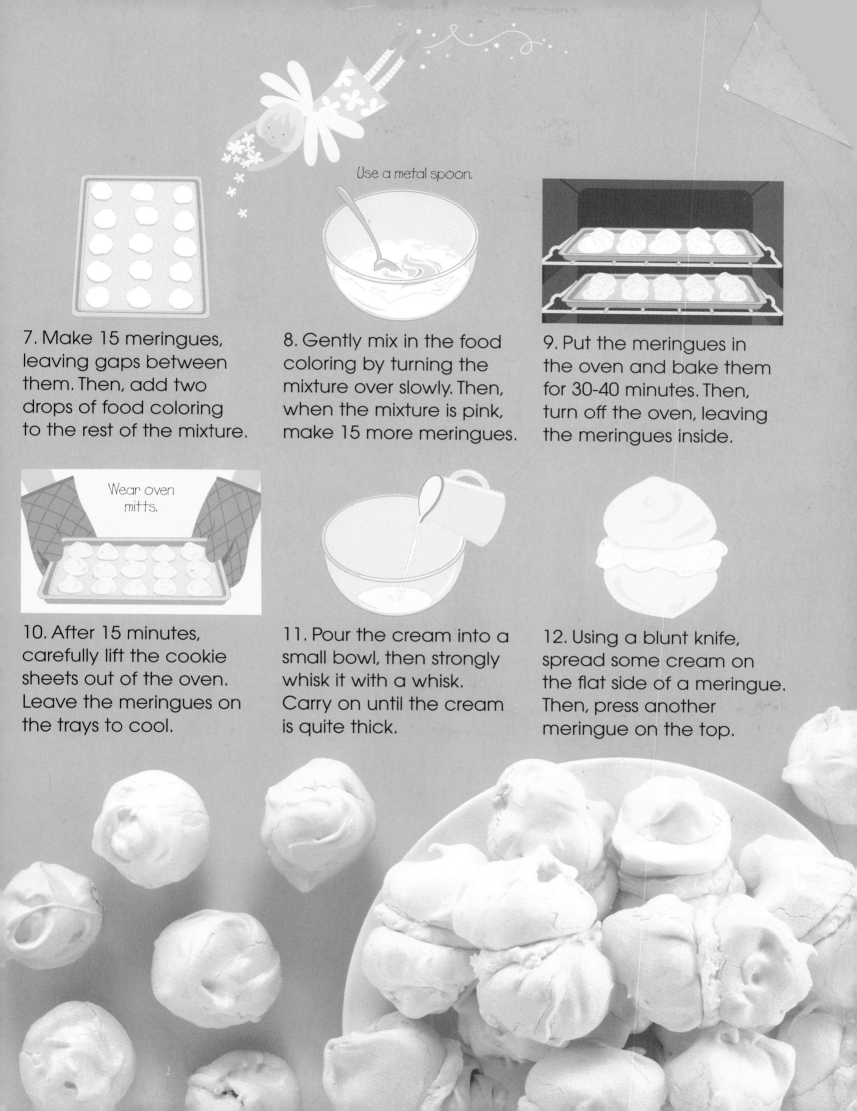

Confetti cookies

To make about 100 cookies, you will need:

4 tablespoons butter, softened
2/3 cup granulated sugar
1 egg yolk
1 teaspoon of honey
1 teaspoon of vanilla
2 teaspoons milk
¾ cup and 1 tablespoon all-purpose flour
3 tablespoons cornstarch
2 greased cookie sheets
small cutters

For the icing:
1¼ cup powdered sugar
2 tablespoons warm water
red food coloring

Preheat your oven to 350°F.

✿ The cookies need to be stored in a single layer in an airtight container and eaten within three days.

The recipe makes lots of tiny cookies.

Use a wooden spoon.

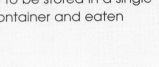

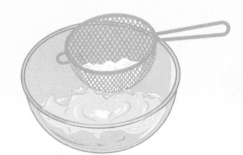

1. Put the butter and sugar into a large bowl. Beat them until they look creamy, then add the egg yolk and beat it in.

2. Stir in the honey, vanilla and milk. Sift the flour and cornstarch into the bowl, then start to mix everything with a spoon.

3. Then, use your hands to squeeze the mixture until you make a ball of dough. If the mixture is a little dry, add a drop of milk.

4. Sprinkle a work surface with flour, then roll out the dough until it is about ¼ inch thick. Use the cutters to cut out shapes.

5. Put the shapes onto the baking trays. Then, squeeze the scraps into a ball, roll them out again and cut out more shapes.

The cookies turn golden brown.

6. Bake the shapes for six to eight minutes, then carefully lift them out of the oven. Leave them to cool on the baking trays.

7. To make icing, sift the powdered sugar into a bowl and mix in the water. Spoon half of the icing into another bowl.

Use a blunt knife.

8. Cover one bowl with plastic food wrap to keep it from drying out. Then, mix a drop of food coloring into the other bowl.

9. Spread half of the cookies with white icing. Then, spread the others with pink icing and leave the icing to set.

Marzipan toadstools

To make 8 toadstools, you will need:

9oz. 'white' marzipan*
red food coloring

❀ The toadstools need to be stored in an airtight container and eaten within three weeks.

1. Cut the block of marzipan in half. Then, wrap one half in plastic food wrap and put the other half in a small bowl.

2. Add three drops of coloring to the bowl and mix it in with your fingers. Then, break the marzipan into eight pieces.

3. Roll each piece into a ball, then squash them to make toadstool shapes. Press your thumb into the bottom to make a hollow.

Wash your hands first.

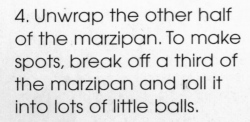

4. Unwrap the other half of the marzipan. To make spots, break off a third of the marzipan and roll it into lots of little balls.

5. Press several little balls onto each toadstool. Then, break the remaining piece of marzipan into eight pieces.

6. Roll each piece between your fingers to make a stalk. Then, press a red top onto each stalk to complete the toadstool.

* Marzipan contains ground nuts, so don't give the toadstools to anyone who is allergic to nuts.

Series editor: Fiona Watt   Art director: Mary Cartwright   Photographic manipulation: Emma Julings
First published in 2003 by Usborne Publishing Ltd., Usborne House, 83-85 Saffron Hill, London, England. www.usborne.com Copyright © 2003 Usborne Publishing Ltd.
The name Usborne and the devices ♀ ⊕ are Trade Marks of Usborne Publishing Ltd. All rights reserved. No part of this publication may be reproduced, stored in a retrieval system, or transmitted in any form or by any means, electronic, mechanical, photocopying, recording or otherwise without the prior permission of the publisher.
AE First published in America in 2004. Printed in Malaysia.